20 *on* 3

Faith, Hope & Charity

An Anthology

Warren Publishing, Inc.

Published by Warren Publishing, Inc.
Huntersville, NC
www.warrenpublishing.net

ISBN: 9780985309466

Library of Congress Control Number: 2012946954
Printed in the United States of America

Cover photography by Katherine Wolfe

✠

Introduction i

✠

FAITH 1

✠

HOPE 31

✠

CHARITY 53

✠

Contributing Authors 79

✠

INTRODUCTION

✤

Faith, Hope and Charity...20 on 3... this title drifted into my psyche, like the remnants of a dream. Over the past year, during my own recovery from open heart surgery, a repair to a 'tear in my heart', I would be haunted by these words.

While driving to work, or in the midst of a conversation, I would think of this title over and over again. It was a mantra that I couldn't shake! It reminded me of being wheeled into the O.R. and having the inopportune lyrics to Staying Alive pop into my mind... Staying alive...staying alive, ah ah ah ah...staying ali...ve...

I had no idea what the '20 on 3' meant, but of course, I had just experienced my own encounter with my beliefs about Faith... that I would get through the surgery successfully... Hope... that I would come out stronger and with renewed energy... and Charity... that I would be dependent upon the unexpected acts of kindness from so many others.

So, here I was, with a title and nothing to go with it. So, as I often do, I put the idea on the back burner of my brain and went about the everyday details of living. Until, one night...

The evening news had been horrendous... just more bad news, angry people, a sinking economy, and people losing their homes and jobs and more. I had trouble sleeping and I had time on my hands. So I got up from my cozy bed during the wee hours of a bitter cold February night. I gazed out the window and shivered as I studied the heavy, ice laden branches. The scene was cold and desolate, much like the news had been. All the light seemed to have been drained from the night, all except...

One tiny glimmer. A slight reflection that settled on an ice covered branch. The sliver was clear and yellow and spread to a deep orange. It was in that reflection that the purpose of the anthology title became clear.....I would ask 20 authors what they thought about 3 topics, Faith, Hope and Charity. Perhaps they would agree to write something and those writings could help to heal the torn places in the hearts of readers, to reflect a warm, welcoming light to a world that had lately seemed to grow cold and hard edged.

Faith, Hope and Charity... 20 on 3 is that collection of essays from 20 authors on these three subjects. It encompasses their personal and memorable reflections.

From health care providers to television producers, from a teenage novelist to, yes, even rock stars, I would never have imagined on that cold February night that such illuminating writing would be right around the corner, there for the asking. Their thoughts on these subjects are profound, funny, enlightening and hopefully will touch that part of your heart that you thought was too cold or too heavy or too torn... and bring you lightness, warmth and comfort.

Cheers!

Cathy Brophy, President

Faith

*"Faith is knowledge within the heart,
beyond the reach of proof."*

– Khalil Gibran

DAVID LYON

✛

Faith — Although this may appear, at first to be a definition, please know it is merely an esoteric passage from one who feels he experiences faith. I respect the rights of others who feel entitled to their own beliefs. And I understand that faith has very personal as well as universal properties. Even while making this disclaiming statement, I intend to lay claim to my experience with the subject.

Time passes between intervals of my life where faith feels more significant. I often express its prime significance when I discover myself at the end of my rope. I might lie still for a while and finger the tassels of fraying fiber at the end of my boldest efforts. The candle beside me burns lower but slowly being made also of fine quality. Then with warm wax at the tips of my fingers I twist small threads of string between them. This begins the process of frapping the fraying fibers at the end of my rope. I should let the readers know that I am not really a rope maker. This moment simply describes where I turn from the feeling of loss toward resolution. Faith fills the void.

In this moment I know I am not alone in this world. I never have been and never will be. All that I know and all that I've learned has been shown to me by others. No one individual could ever provide for my every need, but a host of individuals have supplied me along the way. Each in their own capacity for love, they have shown me the way each day to move forward toward the next. And here at the end of my rope I know it is not the end of the line, or any more dramatic phrase that could imprison me in a moment of loss.

And if you must know, the faith I have is in God. I have placed very little faith in humanity in my youth. And in an enormous effort to reverse the effect I later placed a great deal. I came up very short on both occasions. I agree with the late Voltaire who stated, "If there were no God it would be necessary that we create Him."

My personal faith lies deeper than any philosophy or faith in the philosopher. I have had deep and profound experiences with the Creator. Those experiences could fill a volume of uplifting tales. I have witnessed phenomena that when discussed with practitioners of the sciences had them remark, "You are privileged to have had that experience". My hope is that others too will know they can experience miracles. I believe that God becomes known easily to anyone who will open themselves to the possibility.

Faith gives me something to believe in much greater than how I feel in the day-to-day. Faith for me has become the experience of living within a world where I may be defeated. Faith brings forth hope, that effervescent feeling of renewal when the will is broken. When I act on faith that the world renews itself each day in a manner that brings forth from its earth new fiber, I know it is merely a matter of time before I will again begin braiding new rope.

BEV SWANSON

✛

I sat in the cozy bedroom to which I had often retreated at day's end to thank God for His goodness. We lived in a house I loved in a neighborhood where we had developed many friendships. Life was comfortable. We were happy. God was good. That night however I was not noticing the carefully chosen décor or the moonlight filtering through the branches outside my window. I was reliving the moment that afternoon when the doctor dropped the word cancer into our lives. After spending the long summer going from one medical test to another the diagnosis we had dreaded had been handed down, not to me but to my fourteen-year-old daughter.

Katie was one of those positive, happy kids enjoyed by adults and teens alike. A good student, she had the endearing ability to laugh at her own clumsiness in social situations. Her directness often landed her the label of typical blonde. Her laugh was infectious. Last year I asked God to give her something to ground her in life, something to broaden her world beyond her silly teenage priorities. I wondered if God was answering that prayer through cancer. What kind of path was He taking us on? How much He must trust us to lead us into this unknown valley! I didn't feel fear or panic that evening. I felt numb, but I also felt awed by the responsibility that was being bestowed upon me to be faithful. If God is good then He is good all the time, and He was trusting me with a challenge He believed I could handle. If I really believed Him, He was giving me the chance to show the world and my daughter His faithfulness by trusting Him with her very life. Suddenly I understood Faith. It means nothing when we have all the answers. It is everything when we don't. Faith was standing before me with her hand out waiting for me to take the first step. I knew whatever happened I would not doubt God. I knew the adventure I was about to embark on was the remarkable journey called Faith.

DONNA COLE

✣

I must admit, there have been times in my Christian walk that my faith was not as strong as I wanted it to be. I wavered out of fear or doubt or both. What bothers me most about this is the undeniable fact that never at any time in my forty-nine years of life has God failed to show up. Although his timing may not have always met with my expectations, His arrival proved He was in control.

For those who don't have a personal relationship with Christ Jesus, it's easier to understand how burdened with fear they may be. But how many Christians today live less than victorious lives due to lack of Faith? I once heard a minister say when we stand before God, it will not be what we did wrong that will cause us sadness, but all the opportunities we missed due to disobedience and lack of faith.

After the 9/11 disaster, my husband Steve, a Delta Airlines pilot had fifty percent of his income taken away with little time for us to prepare for this drastic lifestyle change. Through fear, we made decisions, some of which were not very wise, to compensate for this reduction in income.

Without seeking God's approval, we purchased a company in a declining economy that would not only fail, but also deplete what little reserve we had left. What happens when funds run low, when there isn't enough paycheck left to cover all the expenses? Something breaks - the car, the garbage disposal, possibly the home heating system. It's an endless cycle – trying to stretch nickels into dimes.

My breaking point came when we saw evidence the roof on our home was leaking water. It wasn't covered under insurance and since it was a tile roof, replacement was more than what my car cost. After several estimates, we made the decision that our only decision was to leave it in the hands of God. I sat alone on my sofa several days later and cried as I asked God for an answer. It was at that moment that a sweet spirit engulfed me and I heard his soft whisper, "Donna have you seen one drop of water come through the roof?" My answer to God's question was, "No, I had not seen one drop of water come through the roof." And I knew in that moment I never would.

God's answer to my cries was about to set His real plan in motion. My faith, the charity I felt toward others, and my desire to extend the hope given to me was about to be tested. Receiving a blessing from God comes with responsibility! They are twofold, threefold, and so on. They are meant not only to touch our lives, but also to help us touch the lives of others.

Not long after this, the earthquake hit Haiti and our hearts ached as we watched the hopelessness that penetrated that nation. While watching Kingdom Connection one Sunday morning, my faith, hope and charity would be tested all at once. Jentezen Franklin was asking for 100 people to step out in faith and each build a home for a family in Haiti. I felt a tugging on my heart that we were to be one of those 100 people. But for a second I hesitated and thought about our roof. Could we send money to build someone a home when we needed a small fortune to repair our roof? Immediately, I answered my own question. This was an opportunity for us to have the privilege of giving a family a home. In all likelihood, it was their first home. Whatever financial problems we faced, we always had a roof over our head; even a leaky one was better than none at all – as was the case for so many in Haiti. My hesitation faded as I was reminded of God's whisper. My faith was strong; I knew what I had heard from Him, and I was leaving it in His hands. I presented the opportunity to Steve. He never hesitated in his response, "Yes, let's do it!" I praised God for my husband's heart.

We sent the money and out of curiosity decided to have the roof inspected one last time. There were a few tiles that needed replacing, but the roof's substructure (which we were originally told was severely damaged) was strong and needed no repair. Not only that, but after a thorough inspection, not one leak had ever occurred!

AMY DENMAN

⁜

I Corinthians 13:13 the Apostle Paul writes, "And now (right here, right now) abides (or lives or dwells among us)...faith, hope and charity, these three, but the greatest of these is charity."

WHAT IS FAITH?

According to 2 Corinthians 4:13, faith is made up of two components - Believing and Speaking. "It is written: "I believed; therefore I have spoken." Since we have that same spirit of faith, we also believe and therefore speak." And Hebrews 11:1 says, "Now faith is the substance of things hoped for, the evidence of things not seen."

The term translated "faith" in Hebrews 11:1 is defined as "trust," "firm persuasion," "belief," "confidence," or "conviction." But the writer of Hebrews informs us it is "the substance of things hoped for, the evidence of things not seen" and that my friend, requires us to believe. In Mark 9:23 Jesus said, 'If You can?' All things are possible to him who believes."

In my own life, I have found that, "Faith" is a gift of God which grows during times of trouble, doubt and despair. Faith is what lifts us into a higher realm of life! It picks us up and puts us in a place where others may choose not to walk, but they could... We all have the choice to believe that tomorrow will be a better day or that life's broken road will eventually lead us to where we are supposed to be. Faith gets me up in the morning, even when my mind is screaming, "Why bother?"

As a wife and mother of five grown children, I have experienced first hand many seasons where life has appeared dark and uncertain, where faith was but a single word and not a conviction. In my life, I have experienced sexual abuse, abandonment, divorce and paralyzing shame. I know first hand what it is to have depression standing at the threshold of my door, as I have struggled through a marriage where the mismanagement of finances and constant deception has attributed to the loss of hundreds of thousands of dollars and worse yet, trust. I have lost two pregnancies, failed at parenting, failed at many things, and as a family we've all questioned on more than one occasion, why has this "happened" to us?

Yet had it not been for my personal faith in Jesus Christ, and a conviction that the promises God has spoken in His word are true, then I would have to say my life would be quite tragic indeed without faith.

Interestingly, faith is mentioned in the Bible over 422 times, faith is simply defined as trust or confidence in a person or thing, however I believe faith is boldly professing Gods truths and His promises over our life and the lives of others, in light of our current circumstances. And we must live with expectation that we'll be rewarded for our faith regardless of how long it may take.

Ultimately, I am learning that God wants to be the source for all of my needs, and that putting my faith in anything, or anyone other than Him, will always bring disappointment.

MARYANN RUBEN

✣

FAITH – A MIRACLE IN DENIM

"Please, Lord, if I could just have those designer jeans, I'll pay attention in church for a month!" The jeans were fifty dollars. Sarah was in sixth grade. She knew it was vain, but everybody else had them, and she REALLY wanted to fit in. "Lord, I'll do anything! Please!?" *Sarah prayed.* That summer, she worked. She cleaned for the neighbors, pulled weeds, delivered Avon books, worked at her family's restaurant. *She took action.* Finally, she earned enough for the jeans. It took the whole summer. Sarah's hard work and *perseverance* paid off. "It was worth it," she thought, "these are the best jeans ever!"

A denim miracle? Arguably so! The story seems simple and even petty. But that is exactly the point. He is the doting parent who wants to give his child whatever her heart desires, but not without effort on her part. She doesn't have to decide what is "worth it" to pray for. The great God in Heaven is the judge. We ask, we act, we wait. He decides.

Faith in God is simple enough, even for a child to unwittingly grasp. Sarah learned that prayer without patience is an exercise in futility. And waiting around for a miracle without doing anything to make it happen is no better. But when we *pray*, *act* and *persevere*, we witness God's miraculous goodness multiplying in our lives. Just don't wait for the heavens to part and angels to descend. *Pray*, that is, ask Jesus for help. *Take action*, don't just sit there! *Persevere*, knowing that in the Heavenly Father you are fulfilled.

JOHN COLEMAN

✛

Faith, is something that you cannot see with your natural eyes; although you can see the manifestations of it in an individual's life, who has strong belief. Faith is a challenge that holds your utmost inner being together. The Bible states that "Faith is the substance of things hoped for, the evidence of things not seen." Faith helps you through what appears to be insurmountable obstacles. Faith helped me get through the military and college, in the process earning a degree. Faith is something that you obtain within your will to succeed.

Faith helped man to reach the moon. A case in point is when the Soviet Union sent up its first satellite, which was called Sputnik, it became a great challenge for the United States, to compete. So, the powers that be in the United States, using all of their knowledge, coupled with faith, succeeded in making a satellite of its own, and sending it into orbit. With faith, the United States not only went on to the small galaxies, but they circled the moon, the first mission; later on they landed on the moon, not knowing whether they would land on the moon successfully, or even get back to earth, successfully.

The mysteries of life are made up of faith and the opportunity to succeed in life is available through faith, as one reaches out to utilize their faith. There is a Higher Power that gives cause and effect, whether one believes in God, or not. The will of a man is powered by faith within the realm of the Universe. So the mere existence in life, is also made up of faith. The reason why this is so is because "Faith is the substance of things hoped for, the evidence of things not seen."

BRIAN PATRICK CATALANO

✥

PERFECT FAITH

Once we understand we are not alone, we are not alone.

Faith is the force that lifts the weight of uncertainty and the burden of our physical mortality from our meager frames. Without this, fear would consume our flesh and spirit in shadow and disease. Yet, with it, our deterioration can be seen as what it really is: a joyous shedding of this muddled form that separates us from each other. We are not alone.

Only with faith, and not belief, can we find comfort in the truth. Doubt does not reside in this place. Fear cannot fester here. And true understanding does not come without reason—contrary to the age-long debate—because the perfection of our Universe is within every cell and within every breath of our existence. It is observable and profoundly ubiquitous. There are no mistakes. There is no chaos or luck. You can fight and convolute this simple truth to your detriment, or you can take solace in it.

It is not in a book, but you can find it there. It is not in any building or a place, but you can find it there. It is not in a person or deity, but you can find it there. True faith in the divine beauty and perfect order of everything dwells only within us, and within us, we are everything.

MARILYN BURNS, M.S., L.P.C.C.

Author of *Lost No More...A Mother's Spiritual Journey through Her Son's Addiction* and *Now I Lay Him Down To Rest*

⁘

EMPOWERED BY FAITH

I believe that faith is a pathway for us to trust that we will be able to do what we believe to be the impossible in life. I believe that fear is the absence of faith. I was blessed with two beautiful sons in life, Jason who is an attorney in Ohio and Chris who is now my guardian angel.

Chris' life was as promising as Jay's until he sustained a football injury in his senior year in high school and a car accident the summer after he graduated that left him with a broken back. After several surgeries, he became addicted to opiates. Chris tried very hard to stay away from drugs or "the devil" in his terms. Unfortunately most of these story lines follow the same path... lives of crime, accidents, job terminations, failed relations, prison and jail terms, etc. Chris' path was no exception. After he served his two years of probation for a felony conviction, he felt he was strong enough to start a new life. He was hired to wait tables at the Naples Tomato, an upscale restaurant in Naples Florida. My hopes were high for his new life...I really thought he turned the bend. I prayed for him to begin his new life with meaning and joy and my hopes were that he would be the best version of himself.

It was so painful for me when I realized it was only a few weeks later that Chris relapsed into his addiction again but concealed it from us. In May of 2006, he wanted me to visit him for mother's day and my birthday. I was extremely excited to see him but when he greeted me at the airport, I had a gut wrenching feeling that he was in trouble again. He denied it over and over during the week I was in Florida. But I believe God wanted me to know the truth so I could prepare myself for what would happen next.

The last night in Florida I tossed and turned listening to my son trying to breath. He was very addicted to Afrin and blamed it on the allergies in Florida. I wondered where we were going next and I prayed to God to please keep me strong for both of us. I was being "told" to go in the bathroom and reach up on a shelf where Chris stored his towels. I did and found nothing but a balled up tissue. As I walked out of the bathroom, I was "told" again to run my hand under the woodwork on the top shelf. I had to stand on the toilet seat and reach high to follow this divine intervention. When I did, it was there that the tube with drug paraphernalia was hidden. When Chris woke that morning, the morning of my birthday, I told him what I found. He was so touched and began to sob...he said that God wanted him to have a second chance and he was going to change his life. He was very moved by how I was lead to his drugs that he believed were very cleverly hidden.

But that didn't happen...he was in jail just a few weeks later. One of the letters I received described his strong faith in God and at the end of the letter he wrote... "*I sit here and think what I've lost and what I've done to myself and everybody and I'm in pure awe that I could do the things that I've done. But ya know what mom. I have learned a lot about myself and life...good and bad and have knowledge beyond my years. I know God has a path for me that'll affect many lives and I am so willing to get there. Just keep praying ma because I know its working. I love you, Chris.*"

Strangely enough I do think God had a plan for Chris and because of my strong spiritual belief system, I have honored what

I believe was a message received from Him. I will fast forward to the night before Chris was taken off life support. He came to me in a dream and asked me to let him go...*I'm already gone ma*...he went on to ask me to write a book for him...because it was going to be his way of helping others, not a longer life on earth. My faith tells me that was a message from God because I was able to sign the papers to free Chris from his lifeless existence, the following morning. My son left this earth about 5:30 on April 24, 2007 12 hours after taken off life support.

I'm here to tell you that there is something much bigger in life than what we are experiencing in the moment. What we have within us is worth honoring. One of the most meaningful things I've read says....don't tell your God about your storm, tell your storm about your God. I thank God every day for who I am and for what I have within myself to walk the path without my son. My life has proven that if I reach deep down within myself and trust that I have what I need to handle the moment, I will be OK. I have total faith in that because I was able to grant Chris' final request of me...*please write this book for me ma...it is going to be my way of helping others...not a longer life on earth.* I thank God every day for my faith. It is the rope that we need to swing out of those dark places in life.

FRED ERNST

✛

THOUGHTS ON FAITH

As a physician, I have always felt that for one to have good physical and mental health, one had to also have spirituality—a strong faith. They go hand in hand, and you can't have one without the other. As I apply this philosophy to my own personal life's journey and to my career as an anesthesiologist, I see how clearly this has played out.

Anesthesia is a specialty in medicine where we take the patient to a deep plane of unconsciousness for surgery, and then successfully bring them back safely awake. It is one of the most stressful areas in all of medicine. To do anesthesia successfully, you have to be able to handle high levels of stress on a daily basis. In fact, every anesthetic you give is a lesson in handling stress. I personally could not have done this for over 40 years as I did without a strong faith that "somebody upstairs" was watching over me and guiding my every move.

There were so many times in my career that making the right decision for a patient was like standing at a fork in the road and choosing the correct path to take. I can honestly say that my faith help guide me to make the correct decisions. Yes, I made some human errors along the way, but fortunately, none caused any major harm to any patient. The fact that I never had any medical-legal activity in my entire 40 plus year career bespeaks of the faith I carried, and the blessings I received from upstairs in practicing my profession.

When it came time to semi-retire in 1996, my faith once again lead me to my second career as a patient rights advocate. Speaking out about substandard medical practices, breaking the "unspoken code of silence" that exists in the medical profession, and trying to educate the public on how to become a more informed, proactive medical consumer are not always popular with many of my medical colleagues. Without my faith, I could not have achieved this through co-authoring two medical consumer advocacy books, a syndicated newspaper column, national speaking, and radio/TV interviews (over 500 to date) talking on current medical consumer topics.

In counseling patients, I have tried to share my journey and how faith has played such an important part. It has always been humbling and gratifying for me to see faith working in my patients, especially if something I may have said turns a light on for them, and they begin to see things in a better perspective.

MYNDIE MCFARLAND

✛

My husband and I have owned an architectural firm for over eight years and for the past couple of years we have done everything to try and keep it going through this economy. With every day that we try, things just kept getting worse. Not only has the business slowed down considerably but we have also lost our home, which we designed and built ourselves.

There is one thing that we have learned through this life lesson: we have our family, our health and a strong faith. Faith is not just something that you can pull out of your pocket when you need it, but it is something that no one can take away.

MARK C. CROUCH

✤

DEEP LOVE

When in the darkest hour I know 'tis there,
Though deep despair, God's love waits there for me.
One cannot ever go beyond His care,
His love is in the depths, beneath the sea.
If one from off the narrow path should stray,
No breadth too wide where God's love cannot go.
He'll gently lead and guide back toward the way
If only one God's love will come to know.
The highest height that one could ere ascend
God's love would greet you on the mountain's peak.
To every length He'll go His love to send
If one would Christ with all one's heart so seek.
The height and depth the length and breadth of love
Are mine through Christ when I'm born from above.

Mark C. Crouch
05-16-12 MCC
Ephesians 3:14-21; John 3:16; Romans 8:35-39

KATHERINE WOLFE

❖

FAITH IN OUR FATHERS

"Faith can banish fear."
— Billy Graham

When I was six years old—1943—my father enlisted in the United States Marine Corps. We lived at Camp Lejeune Marine Base in Jacksonville, North Carolina. It was a fearful time—World War II—a time of blackouts and fathers leaving to go to places unknown by their families. When my father left, I remember telling people, "My father is "overseas", but I always wondered, "Where is overseas?"

At night on the base, we had "blackouts", a time when all lights were off or windows were covered so no light could be seen from outside. My mother used blankets to cover our windows. We could have a flashlight or low light if needed, but patrols checked to make sure no lights were visible to enemy ships or planes that may be off our shore. I remember listening for the sound of planes in the air, but when I was older, I learned our biggest threat was German U-boats off shore, waiting for a chance to torpedo and sink our ships, which they successfully accomplished on many occasions.

During the day I went to school on the base. I learned to read and do all the normal things children do in first grade, but I also learned ways children could support the war effort.

We could buy stamps for ten cents each, put them into a book, and trade the book, when filled, for a war bond. We could collect tin cans, tin foil gum wrappers, scrap metal and anything that could be melted down to build planes and weapons.

I liked feeling I could do something to help with the war, but my most vivid memory is starting the day facing the U. S. flag and singing *From the Halls of Montezuma to the shores of Tripoli*, the Marine Hymn, then singing the Star Spangled Banner. It gave me faith our fathers would win the war "overseas" and come home. Mine did. In 1945, my father came home from Okinawa, a month after the war ended.

KENNETH BROWN

❖

Making decisions is not hard at all. It's living with your decisions that can kick you in the head. Man up is what I have to tell myself quite often. I know one day I will look back on these days and say, remember when? I will not be mad when that day comes. Meanwhile, count it all joy. But it's not all joy. And remember, I'm a realist. Keeping it real. Believe me, I know all about it not being all joy. Remember that you are in charge of what you think about. Don't look for it to be easy all the time. Sometimes it is easy. Make note of those times so you can go back to that moment. That's why it is not good to get your mind all bogged down with useless babblings. You will hear them all day and night if you choose to listen. We have to get in the habit of protecting what we hear. Some things are not worth processing. The time you save may be joyful.

With MS or most other conditions it pays to pay attention to your surroundings. Knowing what works for you, and when. These are little things that are most effective when kept little. No need for all the drama. For me, drama equals stress. And you know stress is not a friend of mine. So let's not make a big deal out of keeping things simple. Just do it. Life's lessons are not always the way or the ones that you want, but its all-go, just pay attention. I say that, knowing that this writing has shown me, lack of paying attention can cause you to do some dumb stuff. No, I am not going to list all or any of the examples. Who's doing the writing here? Enough said! Keeping an open attitude or mind has its high points. You can really learn from your own writings. I must admit that I haven't written everything I have thought about. It's not that I'm scared, but some things are in what I call my James Bond file. Meaning its information I give out on a need-to-know basis.

There are some things I don't need to tell. You need to know when the best time for you to be creative is. The time may very well not be the same every time. So keep your antenna up. Using your creative talents can do good things for your confidence and self-esteem. Doing this makes you feel like you have contributed to the well being of the world, a small part of the world, one piece at a time. You know, I heard that anticipation causes disappointment, meaning if you don't expect much then this reduces the chance for disappointment. Sometimes you just have to take a risk.

Hope

"Hope is a waking dream."

– Aristotle

JOHN COLEMAN

✛

Hope — According to Webster's dictionary, hope is "to desire with expectation of fulfillment, to wish, to want." I believe every human being enters this world possessing a certain amount of hope. It seems to be an innate, inherent part of our being. To me, to hope is to dream and to try to make those dreams come true. A child hopes he will make good grades in school. An employee hopes to obtain that promotion. A chemist hopes to arrive at the correct formula. A mother hopes her infant will be born healthy. An opera singer hopes his voice will resonate beautifully during an upcoming engagement, even though he is struggling with symptoms of a cold.

Hope is very interesting, because in order to make it work, specific conditions must be met even when it is within one's ability to make it work. For example, if a student expects to makes good grades, they will need to study. To earn the promotion, the employee will need to be a team player, respect peers and subordinates, possess other attributes that are essential to moving ahead on the job. The chemist will spend an untold number of hours treating the structure, composition and properties of substances and of the transformations which they will undergo. During pregnancy, the mother would have concentrated on maintaining good health; so she can deliver a healthy baby. The opera singer allows ample time for his vocal chords to rest prior to his performance. So, their actions play an enormous role in propelling their hope forward.

At the other end of the spectrum, there are circumstances we are faced with, beyond our control, and we hope the end results are positive. For instance, man has no control over the forces of nature, such as tornados, hurricanes, monsoons. An earthquake uproots everything in its path, destroying buildings, homes, trees, etc. One can only hope that they survive physically, mentally and emotionally.

Therefore, regardless of the circumstances we are confronted with in life, we can hope. We can dream. We can wish. We can have high expectations. We can remain hopeful.

AMY DENMAN

⟐

WHAT IS HOPE?

How many of you know, that the choices we make in life can turn out really good or really bad? Often times, without knowing it, we choose relationships, buy the "dream home" engage in business partnerships or make poor health choices that can negatively affect our well being...Spirit-Soul and Body. And more times than not, had we known that the outcome of these choices would have been so bad, we most likely wouldn't have made them, right?

In assessing my own family and those I love, it never ceases to amaze me how quickly devastation, destruction and loss can come into our lives. Sometimes this devastation, loss and destruction comes our way by choices we've made, but other times it's because of the choices others have made. Still other times, it has nothing to do with "them" or "us" at all, but the end result more often than not, is loss of hope. I know that has been true in my own case.

I want to be very clear on one key point as I write about Hope. And that is this; there is thief in the earth today, that comes to steal, kill and destroy. John 10:10 says, "The thief comes only to steal and kill and destroy; I have come that they may have life, and have it to the full (or more abundantly)."

Like many of you, emotionally devastating things have happened to me in my childhood, my marriages, my career, with my children, or with our finances which I do not understand. It's as if a fire has swept through certain areas of my life and more times than not, I'm left standing alone in the ashes of destruction, to grieve these losses. However, time after time, my hope is renewed by two particular passages of scripture. One found in Isaiah 61 and the other in Luke 4. What Isaiah said was a prophetic promise: But what Jesus is quoted as saying in Luke 4 has been made a reality by His very life. Please read those two passages on your own and let hope come back on the inside of you!

Today, you might be in a place of ashes, despair, loss, devastation or destruction and yet, I want to encourage you and give you hope, that you can rise out of those ashes and your mourning, like mine can be replaced with hope! God is not content for us to live without hope. He wants to lift off the heaviness and replace it with something that brings life.

Jesus Christ has come and released into our lives the free favors of God. Jesus ushered in the year of the Lord and He is ready to appoint unto us a crown of beauty instead of

ashes, the oil of joy instead for mourning, and a garment of praise instead of a spirit of despair.

You are not reading this by accident, God is all about second chances and restoration. Where you

have known ashes in your life, I pray you will know joy.... and that hope will rise again.

JO ANN DARBY

Author of Author of *The Girlfriend Book* and *Much Girlfriend Love*

✛

Own your own power and increase the quality of your life.

When you feel your world is crashing down on you, such as your job, money, relationships, etc...It's hard to simply function when you find yourself in that "dark" place! You feel empty, paralyzed and vulnerable to anything and everything. How do you find the strength to overcome?

You must remember that you and you only you can decide how something or someone makes you feel. The most important step is the decision that you are at the point that you are personally ready to overcome. Once you make that choice, your self-worth, self-imagine sky rockets! After you have made the decision you are ready, the next step is to deliberately change the way you think!

When you change the way you think, you change the way you feel, which changes the way you act which reflects your true character. It all begins with your thinking and you cannot live effectively with negative thinking!

You must process your thoughts on purpose. You cannot live backward, stop dwelling on negative remarks, personal mistakes, missed opportunities, bad decisions, etc...Dwelling on those negative thoughts does you no good. When a negative, destructive thought pops in your mind, you must decide to move from the thought right then and there, not allowing it to process any further!

It's like caller ID on your mobile phone, some calls you answer, some roll to voice mail and some you decline. Process your thoughts the same way!

1. I'll take that thought because it does me good!" (I'll answer that call)
2. I'll think about that thought when I... can really digest it" (I'll let that call roll to voice mail)
3. I'll NOT think about that thought another second, it does me NO GOOD!" (I'll decline that call!)

Many challenges we face as women are rooted in our childhood experiences. They tend to affect women more than men because we are emotional beings! Women tend to carry things said or done to us from childhood into adulthood, limiting us from tapping into our true potential! Two of the largest obstacles in achieving our personal successes are doubt and fear.

How do we destroy that dynamic duo of doubt and fear? We conquer them with high self-esteem. I can tell you all day long how important you are, but until you believe that you are important, the dynamic duo will continue to defeat you. So, then how do we achieve a positive self-image/esteem? By participating in something we do very well! Perform the task of what you do well, and then go do it again, again and again. This will raise how you think and feel about yourself! It will give you confidence to try something new, the belief in yourself that you CAN!

After you have tried something new, take a baby step and try something else new! Set baby step goals to reach your ultimate goal! This is how tap into your true potential! When your-self-image, self-esteem goes up, doubt and fear go down, allowing you to do things you never thought possible. This is how you defeat the dynamic duo! Implement this concept and watch the QUALITY of your life reach mountain tops!

See, no one has been down your path and you haven't been down their path! Until someone has walked in your shoes, lived in your world, dealt with your challenges they CAN'T judge or condemn you! You must do what it is for you that move you in the right direction. Stop caring what other people think dear! Do what you need to do to move in a positive direction! Don't forget how far you've come, where you came from and what you've endured to get to where you are!

Remember everything doesn't have to be perfect to be perfect! As women we tend to go through life always trying to please everyone, make everyone happy, make everything perfect, the one person who tends to be "let down" is YOU! It is impossible to make EVERYONE happy ALL the time. Remember everything doesn't have to be perfect to be perfect!

If you are running around trying to get it all done make it all happen then perhaps you are trying to do too much? If there aren't enough hours in the day to get it all done, perhaps you should cut back? Think about your quality of life and adjust.

Handling all the roles you play in life can be simply overwhelming! Here is a tip to help you make decisions on how you choose to spend your 24 hours of the day. You start by balancing; organizing, prioritizing and then you do not compromise on those decisions. Period.

Design your life the way you want it to work, making it all work for you, not you working for it. You must control it or it will control you. Then commit day by day, step by step, moment by moment. That doesn't mean micro manage everything. Keep doors open but make an effort to carefully examine them before walking through them.

Have you ever stood in front of a microwave while you are waiting for something to heat up and watched the time just tick down? As you stood there have you ever wondered what just happened in someone's life that will forever change their life in those few seconds? Do you appreciate each minute, each second of your life? Those are minutes & seconds that will never be replaced, never changed, never undone. Keeping that descending time clock as a visual in your mind as you go through your day can help you to appreciate life. Through the good and bad. Live each second and appreciate each second the very best you can! Remember when you know better you do better!

If you are weak and weary take some time to restore yourself. You have to have a full cup yourself, if you are to fill others cups. If you are on GO, if your cup is currently full then proceed with awareness. Be intentional with your direction. Don't confuse busyness with productivity.

You may have a dreams but don't have a clue how it can be accomplished. If that dream is burning within, keep going dear because supernaturally your talents, efforts, influences and resources will multiply! They will appear, do not give up! You have been given your dream, your desire, and your mission for a purpose! If you feel you are following the pull within and nothing is happening, things may not have worked out the way you thought they would, then this may just be a time of preparation. Think of it as a puzzle, all the pieces have to be there and carefully placed, one at a time to complete the picture. It may take time for those puzzle pieces to be placed. But maybe just maybe this preparation time, this delay you find yourself in, was a saving grace. What you think was a missed opportunity could have been the greatest SAVE ever! What you thought was a good idea, what you thought you wanted may not be the right situation for you! Just continue to examine within and continue to see with clear vision!

Life is certainly a journey... Everyone has a journey, everyone's path curves are different BUT remember ...

everyone's trail, EVERYONE'S TRAIL has branches that bend, thorns to watch out for, objects to step over, hills to climb and rivers to cross.

Every mountain top requires a climb through the valley. That's why when you reach the peak of that mountain, that view, that feeling of victory is unmatchable! Keep climbing sunshine, keep climbing!

MGFL!

Jo Ann Darby

www.facebook.com/thegirlfriendbook
www.thegirlfriendbook.com
www.thegirlfriendlife.com
Twitter: TheGFBook
Pinterest: Girlfriend Life

MARYANN RUBEN

✣

ANGEL IN SIN CITY – A STORY OF HOPE

One night, about three a.m. Nick was startled from his sleep. "Nick!" God said. "Yes, Lord?" "Write about the goodness of your church family," He commanded. "Yes, Lord."

Two weeks later...

I had laid it out pretty clearly before God and anyone who would listen: We are church shopping. It was all I could think about. I begged the good Lord for guidance, day and night. I guess that's why I wasn't surprised to meet Nick on the plane from Las Vegas.

As we chatted like old friends, we realized we live in neighboring towns. We shared remarkably similar faith journeys. I told him of our desperate search for a loving, active church family. Like anyone, we want to feel welcome. The church should embrace the children, isn't that what Jesus taught? We want to grow, as individuals and as a family, closer to Christ.

Nick showed me what he had written on God's command. "You should come," he said.

Two weeks later...

"We are the light of the world! May our light shine before men," I sang in the car on our way to Nick's church. I tried to remember the last time I had heard that song. Was it 8th grade? As we entered the sanctuary, I couldn't believe my ears. It was as if all the saints and angels in heaven answered in song, "...May our light shine before men! That they may see the good that they do, and give glo-ry to God!"

I wept with joy as the pastor began, "All are welcome here! Bring the children forward. They are our future!"

DAVID LYON

✣

Hope — Hope can easily be seen in the eyes of your beloved beastly companion when you prepare them a meal from whatever bag has been suggested by their veterinarian. Their hope becomes exaggerated if they have had the privilege of sampling some of your more delicate fare. In those eyes you will see that they are trying to deny themselves millennia of their developed instincts. Their highly tuned sniffers soak savory smells from sauces and salivating commences while our meals are prepared. Should they be denied a mere bite at a scrap from ones leftover scrapings, they plead with desire and wage fierce internal war against all their instinctive urgings to leap into aggressive acts. They often add their own colorful language to their lament. Instead they leap into your lap as soon as you've retired to your favorite place to lounge. There they can dream of the satisfaction you've just enjoyed as they bask in the scent of your cooking and your adoration. Listlessly they hope that one day... one day... they too will be invited to the feast.

Hope lies easily within the nooks and crannies of anyone's psyche. Our personal ambitions carry us only so far. We often seek knowing not what the future holds for us. One is fortunate to be satisfied with the results of one's seeking. Some seek only to be spurred on by their results for more yearning still. What better striving could one have but the hope toward a better future for themselves and their offspring? It is ignoble. It is God given.

Hope may drift easily in and out of the mind of one who is set against all odds, on a specific quest. Hope has so often been dashed upon the rocks in our history. Hope has been made by many a man a fool's errand with enough force to make man mention the words, "Why bother?" But hastily we can adapt to the lessons we learn by being led into that folly. The cultivated hope of humanity has always crafted great things for its improvement.

Perhaps a within a pickle you lay claim to the fact that, "All hope is lost." To abide by that sort of short sighted reasoning really would be tragic? If you find you cannot trust anything from these words please hearken to this. I have passed two stones through my own beloved kidney's one apiece. During which each bit of time passed uneasily into the next. I pined for the days when I was a young boy, captain of a sailing vessel of one and learning how to pilot a craft. Though I was never beyond the shouting distance of my instructor, I became caught in irons and abandoned all hope. The water's current dashed my floundering vessel upon the rip-rap, laid against an Interstate causeway. I made the decision to abandon ship and make my way up the embankment of sharps stones in bare feet.

I was driven by fear toward the familiar drone of passing motorists. I found myself acting on instinct. It is possible that the error of my adolescent reasoning could have provided horrific, or more likely humiliating consequences, were I to trust them with integrity. I was fortunate that day that I abandoned the safety of my own reasoning and became willing to listen to the directions shouted by my instructor. She commanded that I return to my abandoned vessel and make haste for landfall at her direction.

As audacious as it sounds, I have found hope to be among the most trusted companions on the road of life. I've maintained this tact even when violent winds of change have caused my sail to luff. Just as the wind, the winds of change have little form or reason when they become a tempest. I may trust in leadership when I need to hear it. And I hope for a better and more prosperous future for everyone who makes faith and virtue priorities in their lives.

KENNETH BROWN

✛

IF ONLY

HOPE was all she had left after the fire killed her family and destroyed her home. She was the only one who knew the fire was the result of her irresponsibility. How many times had her mother asked her not to leave candles burning when she went out? Her plan was simply to go the store and get some 'adult' grape juice. It was a typical Saturday night for her. She had her favorite radio station on and wanted to sit and drink some 'juice.'

Everyone was feeling sorry for her, but she was mad at herself. Her boyfriend knew she always burned candles and sometimes left them unattended. Her faith in him not to begin questioning the circumstances was weak, to say the least. If she asked him to keep things on the down-low, what would he want in return? She had never done most of the things he wanted her to do. But now? Even though there was a great outpouring of charity from the neighborhood he was slightly selfish – and a straight-up opportunist. He wanted her to ride to the mountains with him as a chance to get away from all the drama. Just what drama was he talking about? Could there be another way to keep him quiet? Maybe someday, her own heart would be quiet too.

KATHERINE WOOD WOLFE

❖

HOPE AS SEEN IN THE LAST LEAF BY O. HENRY

The Last Leaf by O. Henry (William Sidney Porter) is one of the greatest stories ever written about the importance of hope. O. Henry tells the story of two young women artists, Sue from Maine and Johnsy from California, who decide to share a studio in Greenwich Village, New York. An old painter—Behrman who sees himself as the "mastiff-in waiting" protector of the two women—lives beneath them. Life is fine until November when cold weather arrives and pneumonia strikes Johnsy. As Johnsy lies "scarcely moving" in her bed and staring at the brick wall outside her bedroom wall, her doctor diagnoses her chances of surviving as one in ten because she has lost hope of getting well. When he questions Sue about her friend's state of mind, Sue does not know the cause of her friend's hopeless state. The only thing Sue can say is that she knows her friend wants "to paint the Bay of Naples some day."

After the doctor leaves, Sue discovers that Johnsy has been lying in bed watching the leaves fall from an old ivy vine on the brick wall across from her window and that Johnsy believes when the last leaf falls, she will die. Sue goes to see her neighbor Behrman to ask him to pose for one of her paintings. Behrman, who drinks gin to excess and dreams of painting his masterpiece, can be a fierce man to deal with, but he is concerned about Johnsy and comes to pose for Sue. Sue convinces Johnsy she must close the shade while she paints. Johnsy sleeps.

The next morning, Sue opens the shade, and to their surprise, there is one leaf left on the vine. All the next day and into the night, the leaf clings to its stem in spite of the wind and rain that beats against it. Johnsy decides that if the leaf can survive so can she. Her hope of painting the Bay of Naples is restored. Only after she regains her health does she learn that Behrman painted the leaf, his masterpiece, on the wall and died from pneumonia due to the effort.

Charity

"Every good act is charity.
A man's true wealth hereafter is the good
that he does in this world to his fellow."

– Moliere

PAUL ROSEN

✢

A BOY'S 'HEART' COMES ALIVE

My father grew up in a kosher butchers family in Cleveland Ohio during the depression. Fast forward to a few years before my birth in 1949 where, after his return from the military during World War II, he began his life as a salesman in Detroit.

The company, Brass Craft Manufacturing, was located in a financially challenged part of the city. Before the Thanksgiving holiday, the company would contact the local school for a list of the most needy families.

On a weekend just before the holiday, all of the executives, which included my father, would gather in a snow covered parking lot and pack their cars with gigantic food baskets that included a massive turkey.

This trip my father brought me along. I was no older than 10. As we drove through the streets I saw only dilapidated homes. We stopped at one house and walked up to the front door using rotted steps that groaned under our weight. He knocked on the door and a woman reluctantly invited us in.

As I entered the living space I remember being able to see my own breath inside the house as I exhaled. There was no heat and I thought, "How would she cook the turkey we had brought her." The walls were stained there was no carpet on the floor or barely any furniture.

When she saw the food basked she was overwhelmed and tears welled in her eyes. "Happy Thanksgiving," we said. At that moment my heart burst open and I felt so warm inside. It's a moment I have never forgotten.

Laura Dzubay

⁜

Making Christmas

By the time I got to the fifth grade, I hadn't had many experiences with charity. In fact, I'd say my repertoire barely extended further than glass jars in fast food joints and plastic red Salvation Army buckets at Christmastime. So when my teacher announced that our class was having a fundraiser for Middle Way House, a temporary home for women and children who were victims of domestic abuse, I was eager to help out. I wanted to make up for all the times I'd passed by the bellringers with my hands empty, all the old spare coats I had been too lazy to donate with the passing winters.

Our fundraiser consisted mainly of a class Read-A-Thon. I stuffed enough extra books into my backpack that day to fill a recycling bin, and during our hours of reading I pored into each one, blazing through every chapter while the children in need hovered in the back of my mind. The next week, we used the money raised from the Read-A-Thon to take a trip to the store and buy Christmas gifts for the children at Middle Way House. Into each group's shopping cart went CDs, bouncy balls, MP3 players, Barbie dolls, clothes, even baby bottles.

The ending result was more toys than I could have wished for in five Christmases, let alone one. I wasn't jealous of the children at Middle Way, of course. How could I have been? I only wondered why on Earth I hadn't done that sort of thing before. I walked into Target that day thinking I was going to make the holiday come true for the children in need, but when I left, I found that the trip had made my Christmas too.

EDDIE ZIMMERMAN

✥

I MADE A MILLION DOLLARS.... AND GAVE IT ALL AWAY.

For the last 11 years, I've been the lead guitarist, business director and music director for a five-piece rock band aptly named Charity Case. We play loud rock music in an arena style show and set attendance records everywhere we go. Why? Good question. It is because we are amazing? No. Is it because we are the best band around? Nope. Not that either, although admittedly, we are rather entertaining. People come out in droves to see us because we give all of the money we make to an incredible charity called Grin Kids.

Grin Kids has a singular mission. Each year the organization takes an airplane load of terminally ill or chronically disabled children and their families on a trip to Disney World. We've touched over 200 families and helped them create joyful moments and priceless memories with their children. What a blessing. But really this giving has enriched my own life.

Eleven years ago, I had a newborn son and a very good career in the music industry. I owned and operated a very successful studio and had played guitar with big industry names as well as produced hundreds of recordings. But my life was lacking purpose. Then along came the opportunity to be in this band. From the beginning, it was understood that all the proceeds would go to charity. Previously, I'd never really done much with charities other than writing an occasional check. I've learned those sporadic donations are really the most superficial form of charity. Giving your time, talent and even a little piece of your soul is the kind of giving that is life changing.

The majority of us take so much for granted in this life. We are blessed in terms of health, possessions and choices. It's easy to walk through life with tunnel vision and focus on ourselves and those in our immediate circles. But becoming a father had a profound impact on my perspective and I started to tune in more to others. Coming face-to-face with families that were struggling with terminal or disabled children enlightened me as I witnessed the unconditional love a parent has for a child. It was this love without condition that inspired me to start giving to others unconditionally; to give more than a check. I started giving my talents with no strings attached and no expectations of return. I started giving out of gratitude, not obligation.

Life didn't change overnight. Instead it has been one wild ride. Opportunities that we couldn't have even imagined seemingly materialized before our eyes. No one could have predicted the success of Charity Case. In fact, some days I still look back in awe and shake my head a little. It seemed the more we gave, the more we received in terms of opportunity and certainly in terms of personal gratification. It's a life lesson that I am committed to passing along to my son Alex. There is so much to be gained by giving.

Alex and Charity Case are the same age. For his entire life, he's watched me give unconditionally to a cause that I believe in. He has witnessed my hard work and dedication to the beneficiaries of Grin Kids but also to my fellow band mates and crewmembers. There is an amazing bond that forms between people that unite to support a common cause. We hold each other to a higher standard. We expect the best of one another which elevates everyone's game. It has become apparent over the years, there is NOTHING that we cannot accomplish when we work hard and work together. What better life lesson can I pass on to my son? Alex, "There is a gift in giving, in teamwork, in charity, in doing the absolute best job that you can".

How proud am I that my son walks up to people and tells them "My Daddy made a million dollars...and he gave it all away." I think my son is proud of me. What more can a father ask?

CINDY L. HOPE

✧

THE PERFECT HUSBAND

When I woke up that morning, how was I to know that by the time the day ended, this seemingly normal day would overwhelm me with extraordinary?

My day started out ordinarily enough with a sales meeting. Afterwards, a friend I had not seen in some time treated me to a lovely lunch. My tummy full, I went to meet friends at a home they were purchasing. Imagine my surprise when they presented me with my absolutely favorite snack, popcorn, along with a generous gift card to a local clothing store, all tied together with beautiful ribbon. I thanked them profusely and rushed off to pick up my three young daughters from school and head to church. I was astonished yet again when a friend brought me a huge tote bag full to the brim with perfume and makeup samples! She explained that God had put me on her heart earlier in the day. I was simply stunned. You can probably envision the moment when I walked into my house after church and found a huge bouquet of flowers left by a dear friend. My mouth dropped open, my eyes filled with tears, and I could no longer hold in the overwhelming feelings of gratitude to God for the amazing people He had placed in my life.

Lying in bed reflecting on my day, I realized that God had spoken directly to this single mom's heart. In a tangible way that made my heart soar and the tears pour, God showed me His great love for me. He knew my deepest desires, the things I missed that I had not acknowledged or dared say out loud, things I did not even realize. Yet knowing me so well, He had taken me to lunch, showered me with gifts, and had even given me perfume and flowers, all through the loving charity of others. It was an unforgettable reminder. He loves me, He is my husband (Isaiah 54:5) and He is all I need. With God, all acts of charity become extraordinary.

DAVID LYON

❖

Charity — I have come to believe that charity is selfless giving which allows one to honor their highest moral self. Often people are guided into this act through believing they will receive more from it than they give. I do not believe it is for me to say how one enjoys the fruits of one's labor, be it a labor of love or for earning. And I am hardly in the position to direct the masses. I can only relate to you my experience with this type of giving.

When I was much younger I considered myself quite charitable as well as trusting. I gave of my time and resources in a presumably free manner. But I was often displeased with the results from it. In fact I was most often unlikely to see any result at all, and surely not what I always imagined from an exchange. It hardly occurred to me that I gave with the ungracious notion that my giving would be reciprocated in some fashion. The more I gave, it seemed, the less I was fairly compensated.

When so many people disagreed with my self-perceived benevolence, I was convinced to take a good look at my attempts at charitable giving. What I had actually been doing was bartering with everything from resources to other people's emotions. More often than not the terms were uncertain from the beginning, and the recipient of my charity would withhold something. I still to this day could not tell you what it was I had expected in return. A heartfelt, "Thank You," to them seemed sufficient. I was left holding the full satchel of my expectations.

Through this self investigation I mentioned, I became aware of my fallacy. I began to see where a true understanding of selflessness would aid me in every facet of my life. I thought that I spent enough of my life being burdensome so I sought out to redeem myself through selfless acts. I learned quickly that this too can lead to futility when one caters to the every need of a disorganized gripe. Unfortunately the world in which we live will not become a panacea in my lifetime, though we strive each day to labor in love. Its thirst for charity can seem unquenchable.

So why do we provide charity to this seemingly endless void? We give of what we have without concern for the return. I have lived long enough to see that the poor have no hordes of treasure. Those who lose their very lives to tragedy always do so undeservedly.

When we are able to give we give abundantly. After learning the difference between setting myself up for disappointment and actual charity, I began to be moved toward charitable acts. I would discover myself saying, "It felt like the right thing to do," and meaning every word. Giving becomes best when one seeks to appreciate the value of another individual. In doing so relationships flourish and you will be amused by those you influence. So the cat is out of the bag, (what does this mean)? (one should not keep cats in bags, especially these days where everything is made of plastic. The poor dear would suffocate. Putting the cat into the bag is the actual challenge. They do not want to go in. They pull out all the stops to dismantle the process. So it makes one wonder why it was necessary to put it there in the first place. It makes for one sour puss as you might imagine. Anyone who has tried to secretly keep a cat in a bag will assure you it is quite the challenge. They're usually heard constantly uttering a sad "meowrl."

Right that is why it's best not to keep secrets. Or cats in satchels, or worse your expectations of what charitable acts are worth.

TANYA CANDIA

✠

Charity can mean many things. It can be the simple act of giving - putting money in the collection plate, giving a gift, or spontaneously sharing something. It can also have a deeper meaning, imbuing everything we do and everything we are with an unlimited loving kindness. We are taught to love God above all, and love our neighbors as ourselves. This is difficult to do, especially in today's world where stress makes us short-tempered, and cattiness and sarcasm reign supreme.

For me the daily manifestation of charity comes though what I call the "presumption of good will." When I enter into any interaction I try to assume that the other party has no hidden agenda, has our mutual interests at heart, and only wants the best outcome. Whether at a check-in desk at an airport, while driving, going into a workplace meeting, or contemplating world affairs, I find that the presumption of good will helps me start off with an open mind and a general feeling of acceptance and tolerance that bring charity into my daily life.

MARYANN RUBEN

✜

I AM AN OX

Working as a bartender in my 20's, I never thought twice about people telling me their woeful tales. It's part of the job, right? Trapped behind the bar, I am a captive audience. Tell me your troubles, as you cry in your beer. The weight of the world rested on my shoulders. It was heavy. All the way back to elementary school, I can recall the sad stories: the piano teacher, whose husband was struck by lightning and died, the aging neighbors who felt abandoned by their grown children, a young girl from an abusive family, another from a neglectful one. As I grew older, I would encounter them at the bank, restaurants, grocery store, theater restrooms, at work, and at play. It is as if, I once thought, I carry a sign that says, "Tell me all your problems!" The recurring theme of my life seemed like such a nuisance.

I know now, my sign says, "Welcome, Friends." I have come to expect people's stories in both common and remote places. Listening is my gift from God. Before I knew that, it really did feel like the weight of the world was on my shoulders. Now that I recognize the Holy Spirit within me, it is a blessing and not a chore.

Recognizing our gifts and utilizing them for the good of others, we are fulfilled. What is the recurring theme of your life? Blessings from the Holy Spirit upon you, as you discover your gifts and share them with the world. *Scripture reading: Isaiah 40:29-31.*

JOHN COLEMAN

✣

CHARITY

Charity is a form of love that balances the universe. This balance includes loving yourself, loving your fellow man, and loving nature. Charity helps you get through the day. It helps you on your job, making for more pleasant surroundings. The very nature of love calms a baby when they are fretful. The universe seems to have been birthed out of love, with everything in the myriad of galaxies rotating around each other with perfection. How do we see it? In the glow of the moon; the twinkling of the stars; the flowers in the spring of the year arrayed in all their beauty; with the hummingbird guarding the face of the sunflower; showing true love to our significant others, family members, relatives, neighbors, coworkers, and others.

Love helps the body to heal itself. Love helps the circulation of the blood flow to and from the heart. Loving aids the digestive system to purge toxins from the body; compared to a body being in a state of anger most of the time, which only causes the body to retain those toxins.

Love enables you to understand a Higher Power that you cannot see with the natural eye. Charity also helps mankind to stop wars, and to make peace with your enemies. It aids governments to solve problems that seem impossible to solve. Emerging from a foundation of love helps a child to become a better human being, while learning the ethical norms of society. Without charity, our society could not exist. Remember, it balances the universe.

Mankind is God's greatest creation. Man, who has been extended dominion over the animal kingdom, and the universe, even those unknown spheres we have yet to explore; unknown to us, but just waiting to be discovered. This gesture of love from the Supreme Being, granting mankind this dominion is extraordinary, and should not be taken lightly.

AMY DENMAN

✤

WHAT IS CHARITY?

As a follower of Christ, I have often heard it said that the words faith, hope and charity are the "Crown Jewels" of the Kingdom of God or the very nature of God Himself. Paul says, "there abides these three **faith, hope** and **charity.**"

Now, God could have talked about repentance, forgiveness, patience, gentleness, anything. But He has declared that these three things are of utmost importance and the greatest of these is charity. Do you know why? Well, I believe it's because the Bible teaches us that God is love! (1 John 4:8) See, God has faith and gives faith, God has hope and gives hope, but God is LOVE! So what I want to focus on here is His love toward us, or the charity He has extended toward us and what that has meant to me personally.

Have you ever felt unloved? I have. As a child, I often felt neglected and unloved by my parents. My first husband cheated on me multiple times, lied to my face and eventually abandoned us leaving me with three little boys and pregnant with a forth child. That will surely make you feel unloved. I have felt unloved after so-called "friends" couldn't handle the brokenness of my life or my colorful language, so they judged me instead of being real friends and helping me heal. I have felt unloved by the "church," as a divorced mother of four who was provided no assistance and unloved by family when many cries for help and intervention went unheard or virtually ignored by the very people I'd hoped loved me... yet they didn't in the way I needed them to. Therefore, within my own heart, these events and the rejection I experienced, only helped to reinforce a core lie that, "Nobody loves me, nobody has ever loved me." However this is NOT true, not in regards of my life or yours, because Romans 5:8 says; "But God showed his great love for us by sending Christ to die for us while we were still sinners." And John 15:13 says, "There is no greater love than to lay down one's life for one's friends."

So no matter who you are, what your life has been like, or what awful things you've done, know this; You may have been unwanted, but you have never been, and you will never be unloved. You may be or may have been unfaithful, but you have never been and you will never be unloved. You may have been, or you may be unprofitable, but you have never been and you will never be unloved. You may have been unforgiving, you may be unforgiving, but you have never been, and you will never be unloved. You may be unstable, but you have never been, and you will never be unloved. You may be unreasonable, but you have never been and you will never be unloved. You may be unclean, but you have never been and you will never be unloved. You may have been or you may be unreliable, but you have never been and you will never be unloved.

It is my hope that your feet will be firmly planted on 1 John 4:16 "And so we know the love that God has for us, and we trust that love. God is love. Those who live in love live in God, and God lives in them."

Perhaps today, I have planted in the soil of your heart, seeds of Faith, Hope and Charity which like water, air and food, we cannot live without... for very long.

Katherine Wood Wolfe

✥

Many people think of charity as giving money to others in need. The short poem below suggests that perhaps charity is giving of ourselves to others instead of our money and suggests ways we can practice charity through our actions each day.

What is Charity?
It is silence, when your words can hurt.
It is patience, when your neighbor's curt.
It is deafness, when a scandal flows.
It is thoughtfulness, for other's woes.
It is promptness, when a duty calls.
It is courage, when misfortune falls.

— Author unknown

The story *Feathers* illustrates the first way mentioned in the poem—silence when words can hurt.

FEATHERS

An old story retold by Katherine Wood Wolfe

There is a story of a woman who becomes angry with the wise man in her village and spreads ugly rumors about him. Then, one day, as fate would have it, she becomes ill and decides to call upon him for advice. Knowing how her words have wronged him, she asks his forgiveness.

After a few moments, the wise man, in an effort to help the woman understand the seriousness of her actions, says, "I forgive you, but you must do something for me in return."

"Anything," the woman answers.

"Go to your house, take a pillow from your bed, a knife from your kitchen, and go to the highest hill in the town. Cut the pillow with the knife and let the feathers fly into the air."

The woman does as she is told and goes back to the wise man. "I have done as you asked."

"Well done," he says. "Now, go and gather all the feathers."

"But that is impossible," the woman replies. "The wind has carried them away."

"And so it is with your words. Your words are like the feathers. Once you have uttered them, it is impossible to retrieve all of them; so be silent if you have nothing good to say."

There are many versions of the story of Feathers. The original story is attributed to Rabbi Levi Yitzhak of Berdichev who lived in the eighteenth century.

MELLANIE CROUELL

✤

WHAT'S BEHIND MY INSPIRATION? THOUGHTS ON CHARITY

As a little girl my family members taught me to help people. You have to have that love or passion for people. At some point in my life I wanted to be able to give back to others. Sometimes life will take you in a direction that requires that you help yourself first. It is often tempting to keep the focus on yourself. I know, because I am guilty of that continuously. Now, I try to help others before I help myself. My dream is to help others through example. My hope is that by reaching my own personal goals, I will inspire others to bring their dreams to reality.

One of my personal heroines is Oprah. I love how she gave back and how she was able to encourage her audience to persue their dreams. I would love to follow in her footsteps and I know that day will come for me. Until then, I plan to reach out and help others where I can. I fill my tank of motivation daily with the fulfillment of love, hope, faith and, most importantly, for me, charity.

Faith, Hope
& Charity

CONTRIBUTING
AUTHORS

KENNETH BROWN

Kenneth Brown was born 1957, almost a Christmas baby. An avowed, country boy, he worked and lived on farms, as a security guard and as a supervisor in a furniture factory.

He has one son, aged 27. He was diagnosed with MS in 1990 and is confined to a wheelchair. He likes big tractors, small, fast sports cars and in his own words, he is still rolling on!

MARILYN BURNS, M.S., L.P. C.C.

Marilyn Burns, M.S., L.P. C.C. is a psychotherapist in private practice in Boardman, Ohio. She earned a M.S. in Education as a Reading Specialist and also a M.S. in Education in Guidance and Counseling from Youngstown State University. She works with families and individuals suffering from grief and post traumatic stress. She is the author of several books, including *Lost No More...A Mother's Spiritual Journey through Her Son's Addiction* and *Now I Lay Him Down to Rest*, published by Warren Publishing, Inc.

TANYA CANDIA

Tanya Candia is an international marketing and business management consultant, with more than 25 years' experience. She is a published author of eight books and holds an MS in Systems Management from USC and an MA in Intercultural Communications from the Monterey Institute of International Studies. Tanya Candia is the author of eight books including *Hit the Market Running* and *Build Market Momentum.*

BRIAN PATRICK CATALANO

Brian Patrick Catalano is a former Special Education teacher who has spent the last fourteen years of his life working with individualities with disabilities. He has most notably worked with children with autism within both the public school and residential setting; it is this experience that inspired his children's story, *Touched by Water.* He lives in Los Angeles, California where he is a Behavior Therapist and writer.

DONNA COLE

Donna Cole is a freelance writer, poet and entrepreneur.

Born and raised in NC by a dedicated Christian Mother who taught by example the importance of living a faith driven life grounded in Christ Jesus. Through witnessing this faith Donna developed a passion for telling stories, specifically God stories.

She puts her heart and soul into sharing her stories with friends, neighbors, basically anyone she can get to listen. She considers it particularly wonderful to speak of her Savior, how His love touched her life in a miraculous and intentional way. Secure in the knowledge there will never be a shortage of God's Amazing Grace, she'll always have a story to tell.

Donna currently lives on picturesque Lake Norman with her husband and 2 children and is the author of *Grace Trumps Guilt.*

JOHN COLEMAN

John Coleman was born in Washington, DC and raised by a great aunt, Carrie Coleman Richardson in Lancaster, SC. He attended Montgomery Primary and Elementary School, Hillside Elementary and High School in Heath Springs, SC.

After graduating, he returned to

Washington, DC, where he entered the Army in 1965. He served in Germany for 3 yrs; Vietnam for 13 months, and Korea for 13 months. His state-side service in the military included, Ft. Jackson, SC; Ft. Sam Houston, TX; Ft. Momonth, NJ; Ft. Mead, MK; and Ft. Devan, MA. He served 10 years active duty, and 16 years in the National Guard.

In 1996 he became employed by the Carolina Panthers NFL football franchise, working in the Security Dept and later being named, The Team Ambassador

He has served on many boards over the years, including The Parks and Recreation Commission, Mental Health, The YMCA Board, Central City Optimist Club, Rock Hill Boys Club, and as a Deacon and Trustee at Sword of the Spirit Family Church.

He and his wife, Elaine make their home in Rock Hill, South Carolina.

MARK CROUCH

Mark Crouch is Station Manager of WCLJ TV 42 Bloomington / Indianapolis Indiana for Trinity Broadcasting Network.. He is the author of *Bible-Time Rhymes Volume 1*, *God's Book of Dreams*, *Sacred Treasures* and *Portraits Of Life*. He and his family reside in Indiana.

MELLANIE CROUELL

Mellanie is the author of *25 Days of Roses* and *Sweet Dreams* and several others. She has been a resident in Eastern North Carolina where she lives with her daughter.

JO ANN DARBY

Jo Ann Darby is a Certified Personal Trainer and Group Fitness Instructor (AFAA), Licensed Medical Esthetician, and North Carolina Esthetics Educator. She has worked as a Fitness Consultant for the Teen Tone Extreme Workout Video (Four Crossings Entertainment), as well as a Featured Model in Muscle Media Magazine.

She lives with her husband, Alan, and their son, Trevor (13) and daughter and "Girlfriend," Alana (11) in North Carolina. Jo Ann Darby is the author of *The Girlfriend Book* and *Much Girlfriend Love*.

AMY C. DENMAN

Amy C. Denman, CTN is first and foremost a committed wife, mother and homemaker. She became a Certified Traditional Naturopath after having five children and seeing them all off to school. She has been an enthusiastic advocate for creating wellness for more than twenty years and is married to Derrick Denman, A chiropractor and Wellness advisor in his own right. The Denman's live in Mooresville, North Carolina and is the author of *Secrets to Creating Wellness*.

LAURA DZUBAY

Laura Dzubay is a sophomore in high school, and has been writing stories since she was six years old. She finished the first draft of this book when she was eleven, and this is her first published novel. She enjoys reading and spending time with her friends in both Indiana and Florida. Laura Dzubay is the author of *Room 227*.

DR. FREDERICK ERNST
"AMERICA'S RALPH NADER of MEDICINE"

A graduate of the University of Michigan, Dr. Ernst received his M.D. from The Ohio State University College of Medicine, is certified by the American Board of Anesthesiologists, and has been a practicing Anesthesiologist for over 40 years. Most recently, he worked for 15 years as Medical Director at two Alabama outpatient surgery centers.

For the past seventeen years, Dr. Ernst has served as a legal consultant and an expert witness for both plaintiff and defense counsel in medical malpractice cases. He is a renowned national speaker discussing medical consumer issues that go to the heart of America's health care system and the co-author of *Now I Lay Me Down To Sleep–What You Don't Know About Anesthesia and Surgery May Harm You.* In May, 2008, his second medical consumer advocacy book, *Truth, Lies, and the OR– The Good, The Bad, and The Realities"*was released. For six years, Dr. Ernst authored the nationally syndicated medical consumer newspaper column, "America's Ralph Nader of Medicine Speaks Out." Recently, Dr. Ernst taped his second interview on CBS News "The Early Show" while in NYC. The topic was IV sedation given by non-anesthesia personnel in the office surgical setting.

Dr. Ernst is recently retired from the practice of anesthesia and teaches anatomy/physiology at the local community college. Visit his website at www.drfernst.com.

Dr. Ernst books: www.selfpublishedbookstore.com.

CINDY HOPE

Mother to three amazing daughters
Born and raised in North Carolina
Works as a real estate agent
Teaches a ladies Sunday School class
Volunteers in numerous ministries at church
Has taught manners classes to young ladies at church as well as to homeschool groups
Has modeled professionally for over 20 years, including working for companies such as Ford, Mudd Mask, Wrangler, and Home Depot.

DAVID LYON

David Lyon is the author of *The Great Race*. He is the father to one daughter. He lives with his family in Davidson, North Carolina.

MYNDIE MCFARLAND

Myndie McFarland, author of the hugely popular *Squigley the Squirrel*, began writing stories and poetry as a teenager. Once she became a mother to daughter, Makenzie and son, Ranger, Myndie began writing stories meant for and inspired by them.

Myndie lives with her husband and children in Denver, North Carolina along with their 2 dogs, a cat, a fish, and a turtle.

PAUL J. ROSEN, L.D., L.AC., EAMP

Paul J. Rosen, L.D., L.Ac.,EAMP is a licensed acupuncturist in Portland, Oregon, and Vancouver, Washington, where he is clinic director of AcuNatural Family Healthcare. For information on his clinic and practice and current and upcoming events, visit his web site: www.AcuNatural.com. He is the author of *The Great Health Heist* and *Be Healthy Now*. His newest title: *Be Healthy Now: For Women* will be available fall 2012.

MARYANN RUBEN

Each of us is called to be a good and prudent steward with his or her God-given gifts. Maryann Ruben humbly and gratefully acknowledges that she has been blessed with many wonderful gifts: an amazing and supportive husband, two bright and beautiful children, and a home in the suburbs of Cleveland with great neighbors and schools. As President of Estate Solutions and Fraternal Insurance Counselor, she has been blessed with the ability to help people enjoy a safe retirement and serve others through charitable giving. And, through her role as Stephen Minister, Christian Education leader and author, hopes to inspire those she encounters to see God in their lives, discover their own gifts, grow closer to Jesus Christ and, by doing so, become the persons He intended for us to be.

You are the light of the world. A city built on a hill cannot be hidden. (Matthew 5:14)

BEV SWANSON

Bev Swanson is the author of several novels about relationships and real life situations, including *From This Day Forward* and *Betrayed Loyalties*. She is the mother of two grown daughters and lives with her husband on Lake Norman in North Carolina. Look for her newest title: *Carolina Nights*.

KATHERINE WOOD WOLFE

Katherine Wood Wolfe grew up in Raleigh, North Carolina. She graduated from Meredith College and has graduate degrees in education and Library Science from East Carolina University and has completed further studies at the University of North Carolina at Chapel Hill. She has worked as a teacher and media coordinator in the North Carolina Public Schools and as a college librarian at Chowan College, Wayne Community College, and Mount Olive College. Since retiring in 1999, she lives in Goldsboro, North Carolina, where she actively pursues her creative writing interests and works part-time at Mount Olive College. Her published works include the memoir, *Savannah on My Mind* written with her friend Bettye Clary Toomey and poetry in The Lyricist and other literary magazines.

EDDIE ZIMMERMAN

Born and raised in New York City, Eddie has been a professional musician since 1985. Eddie's first exposure to Rock & Roll came at an early age, listening to his older brother's band rehearsing in their parents' basement. Eddie got his first guitar in high school, and within three years he found himself out on the road with Baretta Red, a top forty cover band. He then joined an all original metal band that went on to sign a recording contract with Metal Blade Records. It was during these recording sessions that Eddie found his affinity for engineering and producing. After everyone would leave the studio for the day, Eddie would sneak back in and rework the tracks himself. Since that experience, Eddie has played on, engineered or produced more than 500 recording projects. Eddie has owned and operated The Playroom, a full service recording and rehearsal studio in Charlotte, North Carolina, since 1994.

His clients have included Usher, Anthony Hamilton, 3 Doors Down, Jewel, Aaliyah, Buck Cherry, Phoenix, Debrah Cox and more. He has also worked in various technical support roles for live shows with Kenny G, Phil Collins, Harry Connick Jr., Meatloaf, Metallica, Pantera, Smashing Pumpkins and Blues Traveler. Since 2000, Eddie has been the Music Director and Lead Guitarist for Charity Case from the Ace & TJ show. The regional sensation sold out almost all of its 250 performances and has donated almost $1,000,000 to terminally ill and chronically handicapped children. In 2010, Eddie founded The Playroom Academy of Music, a teaching facility for musicians of all ages. Over 300 students have taken lessons at the school which features "The Playroom Method", a teaching system Eddie invented and is currently pursuing a US Patent on. He is completely excited to bring his experience and knowledge to the current and future musicians of South Carolina. A guitarist, bassist and mandolin player, Eddie Z resides in Tega Cay, South Carolina with son Alex and his significant other Vicki.

www.ingramcontent.com/pod-product-compliance
Lightning Source LLC
Chambersburg PA
CBHW021345090426
42742CB00008B/750